The Poetic Rantings
of a Mad Man

The Poetic Rantings of a Mad Man

John R. Yergin

Order this book online at www.trafford.com
or email orders@trafford.com

Most Trafford titles are also available at major online book retailers.

Printed in the United States of America.

ISBN: 978-1-4669-0737-9 (sc)
ISBN: 978-1-4669-0738-6 (hc)
ISBN: 978-1-4669-0739-3 (e)

Library of Congress Control Number: 2011962219

Trafford rev. 01/09/2012

 www.trafford.com

North America & international
toll-free: 1 888 232 4444 (USA & Canada)
phone: 250 383 6864 ♦ fax: 812 355 4082

Contents

Affaires of the Heart
Chapter One

Mystical Meanderings
Chapter Two

Mindless Banter
Chapter Three

To all of the women in my life,
past and present.

Prologue

In an open field of flowers,
Bathed in the light of the sun,
Is where I first beheld my angel.
As she came ever closer my heart leapt out for joy...

A dragon raises it's head from the sea,
He gazes upon a city nestled on the shore,
His life is a lonely one.
For in mans ignorance they have killed his brothers...

I hear the cry of a lonely wolf,
Howling at the crescent moon.
His loneliness calls to me from the depths of my soul...

AFFAIRS OF THE HEART

Chapter One:

Hopes and Dreams

A brilliant sunset melting into twilight,
Is breath taking.
It does not come close to the beauty
I see when I look into your eyes.
A midnight sky scattered with thousands
Of silver stars,
Holds Countless hopes and dreams,
But it can not hold all the dreams,
I want to share with you.
A million tomorrows
Would not hold enough time for me to show you
How Thankful I am to have you at my side.
I love you.

Vision

In the pale white light of the moon,
On a night that was full of stars,
I had a vision, a vision of you.
Oh how I prayed for the day not to come,
Least the light break the spell,
My deepest fear was to wake and find that It was a dream.
A memory left from a mind at play.
As dawn broke over the land,
A cold chill ran down my spine.
I could still smell your sweet perfume,
Assuring me that you were here,
As I sat there all alone,
My heart saddened from the emptiness all around,
I wondered if you would return.

To My Beloved

How I love you!
Words get in the way of my bleeding heart.
The love that flows from me would fill the ocean a hundred times.
Being without you, is a fate worse than death.
Your beauty holds me in awe.
You pale the moon in all your splendor.
The look of innocence has never left you.
How can I hope to please the goddess of love?
When I look into your eyes,
I see the burning lust of the beast you lock away.
The soft chiseled features of your face,
Have struck me into eternal slavery.
To touch your cheek,
Is to feel a softness compared only to the finest of silk.
Every time I come to worship you,
I lose still another piece of my soul.
As you stand there before me naked,
The curves of your body so perfect they had to be crafted by God.
The feelings of lust and desire that well up in me I cannot control.
For I am a mere mortal man.
How can I resist the fire in my loins?
As I look upon the sculptured breast of a goddess?
How do I fight the drive of my member?
As I gently caress the soft mounds of your chest,
Your body quivers as I run my hand down to your stomach.
When my hand meets the forest of your groin, the anticipation
of pleasures starts to kindle the fire of your beast within.

As I slide a finger into your worm vault,
It fills the room with your fragrance.
A passion awakens in my goddess' eyes.
The beast has awakened.
Now I know I must please her or give my life trying.
The burning to please my goddess tears at my very soul.
My mind fogs over with her control.
I exist only for her pleasure,
She explodes into orgasm as I look upon her face.
Already I long for the next time she desires me.

Hidden Feelings

When I see your smile, it brightens up my day.
When I'm in your arms, I know everything's okay.
You've taken my dieing heart and given it life a new.
The time I spend with you, takes away my pain.
You don't want to say, how you feel for me.
I thought you would like to know, I'm in love with you.
The warmth in your eyes has pierced my very soul,
Leaving my mind on fire.
Now that I've kissed your tender lips I never will be free.
I'll gaze upon your pretty face for all eternity.

Children

A sparkling glow of a blue eyed little girl,
Gives me the strength to carry on.
The full faced smile of a little boy tells me things will be
better tomorrow.
Such beautiful children have come to me from a world
wrought in turmoil.
When I look into their faces always lit with joy and wonder!
I know that I must be strong.
I must not let my children be frightened by my despair.
How can the woman they love have left us?
Every day grows a little brighter as I am again
Infected with their love.

Anticipation

Bells are ringing in my head,
A fire has kindled in my heart,
A sweet fragrance fills the air.
Telling me that she is near,
Passion fills me to the bone,
Anxiously I wait till we're alone.

Stay

I wonder why you will not stay.
All I want is to love you.
To open my heart and let my riches poor out upon you.
Such an angel is worthy of worship,
I desire nothing more than to hold you,
Come and share your love with me.
You say my arms are a prison,
That your spirit must be free,
And if I held you close to me,
My love would surly kill you.

Fear

The passion in you is trying to escape.
Open up and set it free.
With a wave of joy you shall find the feelings of love that you
are in search of.
I can see the passion in your eyes.
I feel how you quiver when I hold you.
Why do you hold it back?
What is it that you fear?

Roses are Red

Roses are red,
Violets are blue.
I never knew love until I met you.
My heart has grown to the size of heaven
Over flowing with love.

Blindness

My feelings are stuck in a bottle.
I can smell another deep wound coming.
For the woman I love has eyes for a man who will hurt her.
I don't know if I can handle watching the events about to
unfold. Yes she will come back to me after her heart is broken.
I will have to put her back together.
I have to ask myself why I chose a woman so fickle.
Her inexperience in love is why she knows not what she is
about to do.

Hail!

Hail! to the glory of my queen,
I have come to worship her name.
For I am not worthy of her love,
She has come from heaven above.
Spreading only the purest love,
She has filled me with joy,
For that I am in her debt.

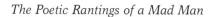

A Hallow Shell

A fowl stench lingers in the air, from the murky darkness of hidden truths intertwined with twisted lies. No one will ever know the truth. Misery wallows with hatreds sword mangling my mind. I bleed from vengeance, you've crushed my heart and I wonder what is left.

Trust

Trust is such a fragile thing. Once it has been broken it is hard to get back. I must not loose faith in the things I believe. Despite the pain that love brings. Some day, yeah some day my love will return the passion I give so freely.

Wings

On broken wings I shall learn to fly up
out of this world of despair.
Silver lined clouds offer new playgrounds.
Like a phoenix my broken heart is reborn.

Phoenix

A phoenix is rising in the night,
A new man is building a new love from the dust of ruin.
Death is but an illusion of life's end,
It is but a memory,
Change has begun,
His will is strong enough for flight.

Red Drum

Red drum, red drum,
How beautiful is my bright red drum.
I can play my red drum with all my passion,
Listen to the sound that my red drum makes,
I will pay my red drum until my hands bleed.
Over and over again I will sound my red drum.

Open my chest and play the strings of my heart like a harp.
Hear my longfull cries for your love.
Miss placed in a mangled mess,
All I want to know is that she is mine and mine alone.

On Stormy Seas

On stormy seas of vial deceit,
I saw your light over the dark waters.
Your guiding light has rescued me from a prison of hopeless
despair.
On the course you have lit,
The sea begins to calm,
Blue skis are on the horizon,
And soon I will be there with you.

Flying Daggers

I must guard my heart from flying daggers.
Less my heart be pierced by a woman's folly.
Many wounds have I endured,
All in the name of love.
Is the joy of gentle caress' worth the emptiness of a love that's
gone dry?

Lost in Love

I'm lost in love,
Oh how good it feels,
With a boyish grin I feel young again.
A high school crush with something more,
I've found someone that I adore.
Thoughts of love that turn in my mind,
I am always thinking of you.

Inspiration

There is a woman who makes me feel all funny inside.
Every time I gaze into her eyes my stomach fills with
butterflies.
She is my inspiration.

Essence of Life

Love dose not bind or hinder,
Love sets you free,
Love milks the essence of life,
To be enjoyed like a fine wine.
Love makes the days much brighter,
And the night easier to endure,
Love makes the roses smell much sweeter,
Loves calms the confusion,
Making everything clear.
Love is the reassurance of knowing you will be there.
Love has crossed the seas of time to bring you here to me.

Cotton Skies

Blue skies filled with cotton clouds.
Loves gentle touch is all around.
People cuddle on sandy beaches,
As I sit and wait.
Longing for someone to hold me,
Once again I've tried and lost,
This time I wonder if my heart can pay the cost,
As I watch my bird return to cotton skies.

Yearning

Lust is an animal of passion, raging out of control.
It consumes everything.
It leaves nothing but a wasteland in it's wake.
Twisted thoughts of paranoia fuel the raging beast.
The smell of sex bends the mind increasing its desire for more.
Self gratification in the highest extreme maims the hearts
ability to feel compassion.
A burning mind sets the loins on fire.
Yearning for its release.
It has no regard for others.
It thinks not of consequences,
As two lustful people engage in violence,
It tears their world apart.

Blind Eye

Blind in one eye, can't see out of the other.
The mind blocks out what it does not want to see.
How can I change things! Most of us plea.
So much evil is being poured out upon me.
Where is the beginning of this mess?
Where, oh where does it end?
My path is blocked by the stupidity of my youth.
It is long past time to tend my unkempt fields.

A Rose

There is a rose growing on the side of a hill,
Reaching to the warmth of the sun.
The morning due still glistening upon the ground,
Coating its delicate pedals like a million magic crystals.
Casting off a soft glow that captures its blood red color,
Making it appear like a ruby.
A gentle breeze has stirred the air.
Peacefulness is every where.
Its gentle fragrance has reached my nose,
In this place grows a single rose.

Broken Heart

Oh my broken heart,
How I hurt in side,
Lord how I beg you to hear my desperate cry.
Take my pain and suffering and cast it all aside.

Thief

Like a thief in the night,
You have easily stolen my heart.
You have taken my love away.
Guard it well my precious angel.
For it is fragile indeed,
Watch as it blossoms into a mighty tree.
Love is in the air,
Can you feel it too?

Field of Flowers

In an open field of flowers,
Bathed in the light of the sun,
Is where I first beheld my angel.
As she came ever closer my heart leapt out for joy,
I can feel a hunger building,
And I shall never be the same,
Dressed in the purist of white,
Her hair shimmers like gold in the light,
Her eyes are full of warmth,
That sets my heart a flight.
The grace of her motion stuns me,
Her gaze has pierced my soul,
From the moment I saw her,
I was lost in pure delight.
For the heavens have opened,
And I have been touched by an angel.

Guiding Light

A calmness has come over my life.
Out of the midst of the darkest storm,
There came a guiding light.
A beacon to deliver me,
From my troubled life.
Just when I was beginning to loose my will to fight.
You came and restored the fire and the passion that I had caged.
For you have set me free.
Filling my body with life,
And filling my veins with fire.
Your enchanting powers have captured my heart.
And I never want to be freed.
You have nursed your warrior back from the brink of death
And I am forever in your debt.
Yes I your champion will gladly give you my life.

Stole My Heart

You came and stole my heart and left me breathless,
Take my love and hide it away.
All of my love is for you.
I have not forgotten what life was like before you came,
I can no longer imagine life with out you here.
All I want is to be in your arms,
I love you for who you are.

Cautious Heart

A cautious heart is lost in darkness,
Blind to the world around.
Deep scares still remain,
From crashes of days gone by.
Poisoned arrows have pierced its trust, time and time again.
Ever so cautious is this heart,
To try and love again.

Open Arms

I stand with open arms,
All of my love is yours,
Some day soon you shall see,
All of our troubles are dropping free.
My heart is pure and purged by love.
You have swept the blackness away.

World Without Love

In your world without love,
I am lost again.
My broken heart took time to mend,
And now it's broke again.
So here I go bottling up the pain.
Shall I always be just a fool without your love?
While all I can do is watch you wither like a rose.
I feel you growing colder,
As you throw it all away.
I am lost again,
In your world without love.
It is not I who causes all your pain.
Please just remember,
I will love you forever.
Baby come back when you have found your way.
I will always be here,
Waiting for your return.
I am forever lost,
In your world without love.

Time and Space

What is it that brings two people together,
Over the distance of time and space?

An internal drive that's pulled me home is the reason why
I'm here,
You left your home so far away to meet me here today.

I never believed you were out there,
So I did not sit and wait.

Many mistakes I have made,
Mistaking lust for love.

Each new lesson learned,
Has prepared me along the way.

Now I stand before an angel,
Pure as new fallen snow.

Now I am wise enough to know,
That I must give you all my love.

I mustn't hold anything back,
And give it without condition,

I want to share it with you,
Lets start our lives anew.

A New Day

A river flows into the sea,
A cool breeze blows across the land,
A child is born with joyful glee,
A flower blossom bring joy,
A broken heart has learned to love,
As the sun begins to chase the night,
The moon gives way to morning light,
A peaceful hush is everywhere,
The hope of a new born day is here.

Woe

Woe be this heart of mine,
No one could feel so alone,
To have a heart as cold as stone,
I have so many that desire my affection,
Yet I lie alone in misery.
Unable to return the feelings that so many want from me.
Through all of the pain it's hard to see,
Maybe it's just my fear,
To open up and let one near,
Is to risk a fate worse than death.
But oh how the heart aches from within,
From many years of suffering.

Lust

Once upon a midnight hour,
Lustful passion begins to flower,
Burning desire manifest.
My little member can no longer rest,
The rage of sex has raped my mind.
Visions of you have made me blind,
Here I stand my love is strong,
How I wonder if I can go on,
My mind is filled with crazy passion,
Lust for you has destroyed all compassion,
Here I am feeling ill,
I have to fight the urge to kill,
The smell of you fills the air,
My mind has snapped,
I do declare!

A Morning Vision

Glowing like a tulip covered in the morning dew.
Her fragrance is sweeter than a rose.
Her skin is softer than the finest silk.
Her pail skin shimmers in the morning light.
Her tender brown eyes betray her eternal sadness.
As she stands on the beach,
The wind blowing her fine brown hair.
The silhouette of her finely sculpted body graces my eyes.
A deep love kindled in my heart long ago.
A love that brings me great pain,
For I know that I can never truly call her mine.
To shackle a spirit so free would slowly kill her.
So I sit here and wait.
Waiting for the day that she takes flight again.
On that day, my life will lose its meaning.
My heart will become numb.
Oh how I will wish to die.
But, I know that I can not.
Lest she shall need me again.
Love has a price.
And mine is more than I can bear.

Pastel Skies

Under the pastel skies of the rising sun,
Two lovers set on a beach.
They feel each others warmth in the cold morning breeze.
To them nothing else exists.
At this moment love escapes the bounds of time and space.
Totally wrapped up in a moment that will last an eternity,
In their hearts they know nothing else,
But the warmth of each others arms.

Glowing Angel

I had a vision on a mountain top,
Of a glowing angel with golden wings.
A weary soul has journeyed home,
To find his angel all alone.

Dream

I had a dream of tomorrows to come,
Days full of sunshine,
And filled with love.
You were there spreading cheer,
And setting my heart a flight.
The warmth of your eyes burned deep into my soul.
I, your champion will defend you,
With all that I am,
Until my very last breath.
You my angel,
Grow brighter each day.
I swear to guard you from worldly harm,
If you would just come to me.
So now I wonder as I wake,
Are you just a dream?

Sadness

I left my home on a sailing ship to search for an angel. Leaving behind the hopes and dreams and crushing the hearts of many. Through the storms of King Triton's furry, and through the gates of Hades. My endless quest has driven me in search of a golden angel. From the mountain tops to deep blue seas, across the flowing valleys to the heart of the jungle deep, she always seems to allude me.

On the top of a mountain, cold and weary, I looked upon the heavens. At the top of my lungs I cried "Oh lord send me my angel and bring my journey to an end". On that mountain I had a vision of a brown eyed goddess with shimmering hair. Of a glowing angel with golden wings, her hypnotic voice as smooth as flowing water. She beckoned me to return home.

Many years have passed me by on my endless search for love. As the shore comes into sight my heart is filled with despair. My home has changed with the hands of time, but then again so have I. Many things have I seen, so much has been learned at a very high price. As I gather with long time friends, I realize their lives have changed little. I know with out doubt they see the sadness that fills my eyes. For long ago each of them had pled with me, not to leave my home.

I have taken a job with little excitement. Much different than what I am use to. Life is already starting to settle into an endless monotony. Out of the corner of my eye I catch a glimpse of a vision that I once had. Only this time I can reach out and touch her. So here I set thinking about the irony. For a weary soul has journeyed home, to find his angle was here all along.

Broken Wings

Tears fill my eyes,
My heart is twisted in pain.
Has my angel fallen again?
A mild sense of paranoia sets in,
I know there is something wrong.
If my angel has gone a stray,
I know that I shall stay.
Please Lord all that I ask,
Is bring her back to me.
I know my love is strong enough,
To heal all her wounds.
So I can mend her broken wings,
And teach her to fly again.
My worry runs deep,
I do not understand,
All I know is that I love her.

Singing Angels

Angels fly to heaven above,
Singing a song of beauty,
Written for my angel.
Heaven rejoices in her name,
All its legends have come to sing.
She is the loveliest of all,
Their voices flow like crystal water,
Pleasing to the ear,
Golden star dust sprinkles down,
Glistening by the bay.
All creatures of earth kneel and pray,
For she has come to stay.

Her Name

I heard a name whispered on a distant breeze.
Calling my spirit home.
In distant lands I have roamed,
Looking for someone to tame.
The genital bonds of your love,
Take the desire away,
I shall not wonder,
So hold me tight,
And I shall always stay.

Come To Me

On the highest mountain top,
To the bottom of the deepest sea.
I can not escape your face,
For it is haunting me.
I can not escape these feelings,
They're slowly killing me.
I have so much to give,
I know not where you are.
Every night I pray,
That you will come to me.

Stolen From the Sea

Over the oceans of deep blue water,
A mighty spirit calls my name,
She has been left alone to weep,
For I have been stolen from the sea.
By a woman who's beauty is far greater than even she.
An enchantress holds my heart,
And keeps it locked away.
Embraced in her arms,
Is where I wish to be.

As Beautiful As

Have you seen where the passion flowers grow?
Have you stood in a stream where mountain waters flow?
When was the last time you watched the sun set,
Over the Golf of Mexico?
Royal blue seas sparkling like diamonds.
And pastel colors fill the sky created by the setting sun.
Falcons float on the air beside a mighty oak.
Wondrous splendors are all around.
As beautiful as these things are,
They pail compared to you.
The joy of life is here.

Love Is Forever

Your smile does not seem to be for me today.
You look so happy without me by you.
If I am pulling you down then I must let you go.
For you are my angel and I do not want to break your wings.
If you must fly, then go.
Just always remember that I will always wait for your return.
I will tend your wounds when the world has been rough on you.
Yes, my love is forever.

Here Beside Me

The joy you bring fills my heart,
While you are here beside me,
I over flow with love at the sound of your name,
I long for the day that you will be mine,
So ease my fears, and tell me how you feel.
I am not the one you need to guard yourself against.
Yes my precious I will love you forever.

MYSTICAL MEANDERINGS

Chapter Two:

A Dragon's Curse

Shrouded in darkness and protected by the sea.
A dragon raises his head.
He gazes upon a city nestled on the shore.
His life is cold and lonely.
For in mans ignorance they have killed off all his kind.
He knows that he, yes he, is the last.
Man understands not how he depends upon the serpent,
Or the knowledge that he brings.
Someday he shall pass on as well.
A sadness for the fate of man falls upon his heart.
For on that day, so to, shall parish man.
He loves man in a way that even with all his wisdom,
He struggles to understand.
He looks upon the star filled sky as he begins to cry.
"My lord! Who hath created all, why must I alone bear your
precious curse?
Who shall be condemned when my will has faltered,
To serve such petty little creatures, who still fear truth and
wisdom?
They destroy all they do not understand.
Yet I love them so".
As the sun begins to rise over the waters edge, He knows he
must return to the depths that protect him.
For he knows if he is discovered man will destroy himself.

Ancient Calling

Out of the darkness and into the night,
The dragon riders are taking flight,
New is the moon,
And dark is the night,
Making them hard to see.
Can you feel the might of the dragons wings?
Can you hear the dragons roar?
The bellow of ancient voices,
From times of long ago,
A time once was when thousands flew,
To find a mate for life,
But now their time has gone,
It's down to me and you.

Self Loathing

Oh mighty Orion.
Where have you gone?
I miss the touch of your mind upon my soul.
I have fallen into a pit of despair.
I feel not the comfort of your grace,
Only the loathing of my greed,
Come back on to me with your fire.
Oh mighty dragon of the deep,
Oh mighty dragon of the deep.

Golden Hawk

I once had a vision
A vision of a golden hawk trimmed in silver,
We sat by the shore of a stream,
This golden hawk and I.
Many things he said to me,
His silver tongue flowed as fluid as the waters of time,
I was mesmerized by the sound of his voice.
He was so beautiful this golden hawk of mine,
Words can not describe the grace of his majesty.
Oh how I loved him this golden hawk of mine.
Come with me he said onto me,
And I shall show you many things.
Over the mountain laden with trees,
Into the valley of silver lakes,
Come with me across the sea of time.
Be thou Hadit, my holy lord,
This golden hawk before me,
I am as a child soaked in his splendor,
And paled against his presence,
In the light of the moon,
Oh how he glowed,
Strange feelings arose inside.
Things I've never felt before,
Lust so powerful to be like him,
Though I knew it could never be.
Be ye as a God he said onto me,
And surely you shall be.

Splendorous

Oh hawk head Lord of vengeance.
Oh how I love thee.
You grant me flight to worship.
I am a spoiled little boy raised on honey of heaven,
and milk from the bosom of Nuit.
I sit by a stream in conversation so rich, with your golden fish.
Oh splendorous hawk I thank you for your gifts of love.
The time of nurture has come to pass,
The time for battle is coming.

Prayer

Why hast thou forsaken thy self?
This folly against thy spirit,
Now thou must untangle thine web of dishonesty.
Thou hast created much hardship for thyself.
Fabricated lies that thee hast handed out,
They only taint thy soul black with grime.
Now thou fightest to get back into the light.
Much heart ach thou must now endure,
To cleans thy path draped with blood.
The time hast came to face thy self,
To taketh thy knife and cut out the evil thou hath wrought.
Help me o mighty God.
Who hath created all.
Grant me thy wisdom to do thy work,
Chargeth me with thy holy task.
Amen

Father

Holy father who art within,
Holy Father who art with out,
Bless thy son and open my eyes,
Help me to claim that which is mine.
Thy holy inheritance is rich with love,
Show me father, the path of life.
The rituals of old,
The rituals of Nu,
A time to ruin,
A time to claim,
Centuries pass with rot and decay.
I was born on this day,
I was born to live,
I was born to fight.
To take the name of my father plight,
Rich with glory and full of honor,
Take me to thy bosom of masculine power,
Thine time has come for me to raise,
Glory be my fathers name,
Glory to the house of light,
Glory to the house of fire,
Exalt thy name of your son,
That I may bring you glory.

A Pale Reflection

Holy is your wisdom, full of divinity.
For I am a pail reflection of you.
Shine down on your faithful servant.
Illuminate my path that I may return to you.
I am broken and full of distraught.
Severed from my god,
For the chance of reunion.
I stand before the gates of heaven,
Humbling myself to your judgment.
I ask not for mercy or pity,
Yes my god, I reek with sin.
I stand before you bound and repressed.
I beg you my lord,
Show me how to be free.
That I may serve you with all that I am.
Cast me into the lake of corpses,
If you find that I am not worthy.
Much troubled ground have I conquered,
Unyielding is my hearts desire to stand up,
And rise from my self created hell.
That me and my god should become one.
Yes that I may rise and shout,
I am one of the chosen, we are the gods.

Worship Our Lady

Come to me my love, that I may love you.
The petulance that is in me shall leave.
You my mate, are the only one that can make me whole.
Take my heart and flee my love.
Show me the tops of the mountains, and the bottom of the sea.
Only with you, can I turn the desert into rich lands
that brings forth life.
Without you, I am the cold of deep space.
Come my love, let us worship our lady Nuit.
Let the continuous one of time and space,
Join us in ecstasy.
That we may awaken the snake of joy
and transcend into heaven eternal.

Desire Another

What happens to a soul?
What happens when you are with one yet desire another?
Why do we seek something better?
Even when we already have the best.

Modern Day Crusade

Over a hill on a horse of steel,
Sir Knight comes riding in.
A breed of man long since dead.
His heart is filled with valor.
On a quest to fix the wrongs,
Of peasants harmed all along his way.
He brings light to a world that's gone a stray.
Pride and purpose fills his mind,
On a modern day crusade.
Days of old have come and gone,
Four centuries late is he.
Corruption rules the world,
Where Camelot use to be.
His Mercedes shimmers in the light of a new born day,
His enemies mass in numbers,
All along his way.
They fear the knowledge he brings,
And the changes that will be.
So they plot against him,
To keep their fantasy.

Escape

Oh how I long to flee into the woods.
To a peaceful sanctuary unspoiled by man.
Where money has no place,
And corruption does not exist.
I would build a cabin.
That I may live off the land,
Returning to simpler things,
That most of us have forgotten.
I only wish to escape the poverties of man.
I desire the riches that mother earth provides.
For I have lost my spirit, to the prisons of man.
The hope of salvation sounds so grand.
Most holy mother do you hear my plea?
I wish to end this senseless self destruction.
Oh mighty mother teach me!
What is the meaning of my life?

Abyss

Oh lord my God,
What is this misery I have befallen?
Do you find me worthy,
To transcend the dark night of the senses?
Purge me oh graceful lord,
Cleanse me of all that is impure,
And purify my heart.
Leave only an undying love for you.
Yes lord I know that I am a retched beast.
I beg of you to purge my soul,
Make me ready oh lord,
To cross the dark night of the soul.

Lost

Gazing upon a moon lit sky,
Hope and dreams are held up high,
I praise the lord for what I have,
Grant me wisdom to walk your path,
Send me lord a guiding light,
Your humble servant is lost tonight.

Blinded

Once upon a midnight furry.
Sky so black and full dreary.
One blind soul lost in darkness.
Steps forth on a hidden path.
Surrounded by the stench of death.
Blinded by a lust for knowledge.
Impure thoughts are running ramped.
Blasphemy against thyself starts to shatter.
The deepest desire for a love that I cannot feel.
A thirst for you that will not be quenched.
Another soul has been cast away.
The grace of God has left today!

Who Made Who

Oh God help me to understand,
All I wish to know is who made who?
Was it I who made you ?
Or did you make me?
Did I grant you the power to control the universe?
Or was it yours all along?
Many scriptures have been left behind.
You seem to change to the needs of time.
Hear the plea of your fearful servant.
Enlighten me, oh lord!

Nature Of Man

The ways of nature are savage indeed!
To eat!
Or be eaten!
Is the call of the wild.
The strong will survive,
The weak shall feed the vulture!
By a stream an antelope stops to drink.
Only to find death in the jaws of a tiger!
Out on the plains a lion dies of starvation!
From too many missed kills.
In the cold of winter!
Half a herd of deer,
Lie rotting from lack of food!
A baby blue jay falls from its nest!
Into the clutches of a bob cat.
LOOK AROUND YOU!
And you will see,
The fabric from witch man was cut.
It is very plan to see,
Man has left nature,
But nature has not left man.

Yell Across

To yell across an open holler,
Hear your voice echo loudly,
To catch a glimpse of Wood Nymphs dancing,
See the Gnomes work with purpose.
Playful Elves that please the ear,
Water Sprits skate on waters near,
Air Spirits fill the sky,
A fire Sprite dazzles awe bound eyes,
With all these things you finally see,
You can speak with the gods upon the breeze.

A Dragons Curse

Original
7-17-95

A dragon raises it's head from the sea,
He gazes upon a city nestled on the shore,
His life is a lonely one.
For in mans ignorance they have killed his brothers, and he,
yes he is the last.
Man understands not how he depends upon the serpent of
knowledge.
Some day he to shall pass on, a sadness fills his heart,
On that day man shall parish.
He loves man in a way that even all his wisdom can not explain.
He looks to the sky and cries "my lord!
Who hath created all.
Why must I be condemned to serve those who hate me?
With out me, man is dumb.
They fear truth and wisdom, yet I love the feeble little
creatures."
As the sun begins to rise over the waters edge,
He knows he must return to the depths that protect him.
For he knows if he is discovered, man will destroy himself.

MINDLESS BANTER

Chapter Three:

Loneliness

I hear the cry of a lonely wolf,
Howling at the crescent moon.
His loneliness calls to me from the depths of my soul.
Yes I too feel a lump in my chest,
And I call it despair!
I know not what pains this glorious beast.
I can only reflect upon my own selfish desire.
I fell in love with a woman,
Who desires no love, only lust!
She savagely tears at my heart,
To quench her thirst for blood!
Every day she laps the life from my soul,
Making my body weak.
Soon my heart will die,
And she shall cast me aside,
With a fit of vicious rage!
Yes!
I welcome this death!
For it shall end my pain.

Running Ramped

There is a fire burning deep inside,
It makes you feel so alive.
To strike the spark will make you wiggle,
To ignite the blaze,
Will release your passion.
Flowing out of control,
And running ramped.

Her Name

Original

I heard her name whispered,
on a distant breeze.
Calling my free spirit home.
From distant lands I have roamed,
looking for one to tame me.
The gentle bonds of your love take away the desires to wonder.
Hold me tight and I shall never leave you.

Together

Open your eyes and you shall see,
A love that is stronger than time.
The longer we are together,
The stronger our love will grow.
Come with me to a place,
That only our hearts can go.
A world that knows no fear,
And has no place for despair.
An angel from heaven has come to me,
To release my heart from bondage.
Your beauty has enchanted me,
Beckoning my soul to follow where ever you may go.
The pain of years gone by,
Is fading from my memory.
All I know is what tomorrow may bring,
Now that I have you beside me.

Carry On

Carry on my way ward son,
there is so much you have left undone.
The time has come to bring an end,
To all of the your tangled messes.
Clean up your past,
To open doors,
That tomorrow is sure to bring.
A bright future lays before you,
After cleaning up your past.
It is your destiny to control your path,
And not the hand you've been delt.
It is time to use what you've learned,
For life is your initiator.

Reaper

Hail to the reaper who comes for my soul.
I smell death upon the winds of change.
The magician is gathering his army of demons,
To wager war with the mistress of hell.
Soon the earth will be scared and battered,
And soaked with the blood of many.
For vengeance is blind and has no mercy,
Killing all who get in his way.
It is a pity this monstrosity of fowl play,
That leaves lives broken and loathing.

Roses are red, violets are blue.
Gunpowder stinks a lot like you.

Tick-Tock

Tick-tock, tick-tock,
Echoes the sound of the co-co clock,
Rattling around inside my head.

Tick-tock, tick tock,
The only sound in the house,
Straining my sanity, driving me mad.

Tick-tock, tick-tock,
Nobody around but me,
Come out little birdie and we shall play.

Tick-tock, tick-tock,
Waiting for twelve to strike,
Watching, watching endlessly.

Tick-tock, tick-tock,
I heard somebody knock,
Look out the window so I can see.

Tick-tock, tick-tock,
Oh what do I see,
The reaper has come for me.
Cuckoo, cuckoo, cuckoo, cuckoo.

The Sands of Time

The sands of time keep flowing,
Endlessly leading into tomorrow.
How argent are we to think we can affect tomorrow,
When we can't even change yesterday.
The over whelming truth is we came from the universe,
And not the universe from us.
The only thing we can do,
Is try to see the plans laid out by God,
Or the universe.
Which ever is in power.
Where are we going?
Where are we from?
What difference do I make?

A Time

A time to fly
A time to play
A time to live
A time to die
The later is not today.

Bedroom Window

Looking out my bedroom window,
To wish upon a distant star,
Twinkling dimly from so far,
Like a diamond in the sky,
You are where I wish to fly,
Up into space away from home,
That is where I want to roam.
Your majesty has beckoned me,
This is why I wish to flea.
From the earth wrought in sorrow,
Trying to build a new tomorrow,
Father time just toys with us,
While we sit and make a fuss,
Growing older and much bolder,
Feeling heart break in the air,
Makes me wonder if you care.
Looking out of my bedroom window.

Silence

Silence fills the air around,
A felling of tiredness over whelms me.
Where do I go?
How do I escape these feelings?
Do I drift across the seas,
To look for a new start?
Should I end it with a bullet centered on my heart?
Is there such a thing as true happiness?
Is life all a blend of bitter?
With just enough sweet to keep us hoping along?
How much is one person supposed to endure?
Whether it is a hunger for food,
Or hunger for the return of a lost child.
Ouch my heart is sick,
There is nothing that anyone can do!

Writer's Block

A hush has fallen across my brain.
The words do not want to flow.
Labored thoughts are racking my mind,
Filling my head with fire.
For the words must flow,
It hurts to hold them in,
They pierce right through my soul.
The words must come or I shall crack open my head,
And scoop them out.
That would be pretty messy!

Just Hold Me

With all my love
to the light of my life,
Oh how happy you have made me.
Just hold me for a while,
Close to your chest
So the sound of your heart fills my ear.

My Life

Something has happened to me.
My life has changed so much,
I no longer know it.
Some is for the worse,
But most is for the better.
One thing is for sure,
My choices now are affected by my past.

Lost Child

To have lost a child is pain without end.
To have lost three is a living death.
To take my children is to take my life.
To fall to hell would be much more welcome.
I must rise above all this despair.
I will learn to live again.
I must remember my children will some day return.
I will look onto that day with joy.

My Rose

I have a rose,
So delicate is my rose.
I must hide my rose,
I must hide it away from all.
Lest it's delicate peddles be hurt,
Or its sweet fragrance be envied by vandals.
It's blood red peddles are perfect without flaw.
Look how it shimmers in the morning dew.

Leave a Message

I have gone away to distant planes,
Letting my spirit wander,
When I depart from my angel,
And my journey leads me home.
I will return your call.

Orchid

I have found an orchid pure and white.
See how it shimmers in the moon light.
A silver glow can be seen,
Coming from all around.
There I stand in a small clearing.
Gazing upon its beauty.
Into a gentle trance I have fallen.
At piece with my mind and soul.
For a brief moment,
I have forgotten who I am.

Mirror On The Wall

Mirror, mirror on the wall,
Why does your reflection deceive me?
I see a man who everyone loves,
I see a man I hate.
They tell me I am wonderful,
My heart is full of love.
They tell me that my eyes are warm,
And I am the companionate one,
But I feel a darkness in my soul,
Because my life is just a lie.

Flake of Snow

There is a crystal on a flower,
A little flake of snow.
I look around and see them falling everywhere,
To the ground they float with ease,
Staking one by one.

Oceans of Hatred

Oceans of hatred,
Mountains of deceit,
Where did it begin?
Where will it end?
Too many lies to count!
They have twisted my life.

Free

Let us go to the blue ridge mountains,
Where the water is pure and my spirit is free.
Animals still roam unhindered by man.
I feel a need, a need to flee from my oppression.

Time Again

I woke up this morning with my mind in a haze.
Images of days gone by ringing in my head,
So much has been lost and so much has gained,
In a whirl wind I call your name.
People come and many go,
Never to be heard from again.
Selfish desires poison friendships,
Time and time again.
I look at the emptiness all around,
Noting my lack of despair.
A seed of life has begun to grow,
Taking root in my soul.
Yes, once again it is time to build a world a new.

Hearts of Glass

Two hearts fly off among the clouds,
Joined together by love.
See how they sparkle in the light of love,
These fragile hearts of glass.

Seize the Day

Seize the day to make things happen,
Only you control your destiny.
Where you go and where you've been,
Are results of your own decisions.

Thank You Lord

Thank you lord for my will to live.
Guide me through this world of misery,
Back into your light.
Let your will be done.
For your will is my true will of purpose.
Help me lord not to restrict or oppress.

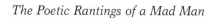

Blind Wrath

Blind Wrath know no limits,
Poison runs to the bone.
A venomous viper is about to strike at my soul.
If I am true and quick with my blade,
I shall lop off its head and kill the beast that poisons me.

Gum Drop Trees

Gum drop trees and candy canes.
Life is sweet indeed.
Baby Ruth's and Butter Finger's,
Dancing on my brain,
Chocolate chips and Oreos,
Falling down like snow.

Bloody Fields

Onward bold faced soldier going off to war,
Bloody fields with shattered flesh have made you hard and cold.
Your heart has become as cold as the steel you carry.
Bringing forth the end of life in violent fits of light,
Living bodies spraying lead in orchestrated rituals of death.
As hidden faces lurk in shadows,
Polishing blades of steel.

Leviathan

Wallowing in the depths of unbridled hatred.
Filled with mass contempt for all that is woman.
Ate up with furry by one woman alone.
I fall to hells worm of disease.
How can one so pretty induce such violent fits of vomiting?
Her illusion of innocence covers a vile core of loathing within.
I fear I have slept the in the bed of a leviathan.
Loosing my soul to damnation.
This vile creature has pumped me full of pride.
Now I am unable to cry to my God for salvation.

Pride

Here I sit, coveting a machine.
Many parts she has glossed over in red.
Yes, how I depend upon her.
Much time has been spent keeping her clean.
Why do I cherish you so?
I look at you with great emotion.
Quite often I find myself talking to you about life's problems.
With childish pride I show you off.
I would morn you if lost.
Now I sit here with a wounded spirit.
Falling to the sin of pride.
Lavishing myself in much gluttony.
Life is to short.
There is so much to accomplish.
I have no time for materialistic folly.
Good bye.
I lay you to rest.
For the time has come.
For me.

Things

So much has happened.
Things are lost.
Things are found,
Things are born.
While others die.
A girl was found.
And one ran away.
Memories play funny games inside my head.
Life has a way of passing us by.

Prophecy

Hear me, hear me,
A prophecy revealed,
The ground will shake,
A thunder peal,
The death of many you will see,
Alaska with palm trees,
Egypt's jungles are dense,
Nairobi's navy is vast.
Dolphin's speak of philosophy,
While whales take over France,
THE END OF THE WORLD IS NEAR!
Perhaps in a thousand years,
People will tremble with fear.
As the ramblings of a mad man,
Are viewed as a prophecy.

Biography:

My name is John Yergin. I live in Indianapolis with my wife Connie. I served in the U.S. Navy from 1990 to 1995. I am a full time auto mechanic who has enjoyed reading and writing poetry for many years. After years of persistent requests from friends and family, I have decided to publish my work. This is the first book of three. This body of work covers the early years, a time period from 1990 to 1998. Although my earlier works where a bit simpler in form and structure, they are still some of my personal favorites. This body of work encompasses a time in my life full of great turmoil.

John R. Yergin